Mother in Summer

Mother in Summer

Susan Hahn

TRIQUARTERLY BOOKS
NORTHWESTERN UNIVERSITY PRESS | Evanston, Illinois

TriQuarterly Books
Northwestern University Press
Evanston, Illinois 60208-4210

Printed in the United States of America

10 9 8 7 6 5 4 3 2 1

ISBN 0-8101-5129-4 (cloth)
ISBN 0-8101-5130-8 (paper)

Library of Congress Cataloging-in-Publication Data

Hahn, Susan.
    Mother in summer / Susan Hahn.
        p. cm.
    ISBN 0-8101-5129-4 (alk. paper) — ISBN 0-8101-5130-8 (pbk. :
alk. paper)
    1. Parent and adult child—Poetry. 2. Terminally ill parents—
Poetry. 3. Mothers and daughters—Poetry. 4. Cancer—Patients—
Poetry. 5. Mothers—Death—Poetry. I. Title.
    PS3558.A3238 M68 2002
    811'.54—dc21
                                            2002001620

The paper used in this publication meets the minimum requirements of the
American National Standard for Information Sciences—Permanence of
Paper for Printed Library Materials, ANSI Z39.48-1984.

For Stuart Dybek and Edward Hirsch

To Her

The sun was shining on the sea,
Shining with all his might:
He did his very best to make
The billows smooth and bright—
And this was odd, because it was
The middle of the night.

—Lewis Carroll

Contents

lacrimosa

Acknowledgments

Grateful acknowledgment is made to the editors of publications in which these poems, or versions of them, first appeared:

The American Poetry Review: "Petit Point I"

The American Scholar: "Relief"

The Antioch Review: "Malignancy in Late May"

Boulevard: "Bald," "Conclusion I," "Gone," "The Interior of the Sun III," "*In the Beginning . . .* ," "Muff . . . ," "Perihelion" (second and third sections)

The Connecticut Review: "Cycle of Sound," "Mother in Summer III"

88: A Journal of Contemporary American Poetry: "Petit Point II," "Petit Point III"

Green Mountains Review: "Bulb," "Head," "Red"

The Kenyon Review: "Guardian"

Michigan Quarterly Review: "Conclusion III," "Heat," "Reentering the Scar"

The North American Review: "The Interior of the Sun II"

Poetry: "The Baobab Tree I" ("The Baobob Tree 1995"), "The Baobab Tree III" ("The Baobob Tree 1996"), "Frigid" ("Frigid 1996"), "Larch" ("Frigid 1994"), "Perennial"

Shenandoah: "Perihelion" (first section)

Southwest Review: "Lizard"

"Lizard" appeared in *The Pushcart Prize XXIV: Best of the Small Presses* (Pushcart Press, 2000).

"Perennial" appeared in *Illinois Voices: An Anthology of Twentieth-Century Poetry* (University of Illinois Press, 2001).

Mother in Summer

pathétique

Mother in Summer I

Here, the Hardy Gladioli with their delicate
butterfly florets surround her
as do the Blue Ribbon Dutch Iris bulbs
that live and multiply for years,
their cuttings lasting so long in the vase—
just like *forever* becomes her face.
She borders my life,
dependable as the garden
lilies. I listen to the trumpets
of their sweet yellow throats—the music
of their silent voice.
We are in the heat of deep summer
and she sits so young and quiet
in the painted pastel
lawn chair, while Green Magic
hybrids with their pure white petals
assert themselves against the shade.
Their perfection protects us,
while I poke

my small fingers through
the cutout design in the steel seat
I've crawled under to touch her.
My back is to the ground.
She jumps. We laugh.

We are not yet old:
Golden Splendor, Rose Fire, Sterling Star,
Enchantment, cluster near us
in this extravagance of color.
She wears a crimson chemise
and her hair flames
equal to the sun.
I wrinkle my pink pinafore
as I lie in the fleshy
grass, turn over, tickle my face
against the weeds. We are surreal
in this light. We are surreal
with all this bright.

Fever

The inside of the lily isn't calm,
the sun has singed its center.
I touch its tender knobs
which lie exposed under
the eye of raging fire.
No breeze or balm revives
its once trumpet form.
Its muscled walls
are still thick, but disease
afflicts the flower.
In the mirror I see the result—
its swell and fall out of itself.

Malignancy in Late May

The ground is too lush, too tumorous,
the tulips too anxious in their push
to lick the sill—violent
purples, new bruises, swell against
the already cracked and fragile
glass. Will it break

apart—that self that contains the wild
cell? Soon the full-blown flowered
lump will appear in the crevice
of your neck. I'll watch you watch
the doctor finger the florid node.
How he'll cut into
the story, tell you the rest

of your life. You'll put the petit
point down. Perhaps forever, never
finishing the picture. *I want it.*
How I love the benign tea rose
you've drawn onto the fabric.
It is so safe, unlike what's going
on with the large-tongued

petals that bend every which way
with the wind—wag and over-
heat in the metastasized grass.

Bulb

Ten years the bulb keeps
dormant in your neck,
ten years we dig our nails into
the dirt, plant Snowdrops,
Dwarf Irises, Grape Hyacinths.
We live according to the catalog,

not the doctor's smudged
report. Outside, the peonies burst
into their huge bouquets. Inside,
wild cells erupt—*particle sections*
show several large-sized
lymphoid aggregates with vague
germinal centers—buds that can-
not contain themselves in the early
summer heat. The rain makes everything
too green. I want to scream

at the thickening
grass to give me my mother
back, although you are
still here and the chemotherapy
has not begun again.
Clumps of your hair have not yet fallen

into my hands, but we've started
to speak once more of wigs and scarves.

How tired you are as we talk across
the kitchen table. Only, for now,
I don't have to cry past

the stone, the out-of-control
growth racing every which way—
forever coming back,
no matter how we hack at it.

Cure

Inside, acid rain awoke
the indolent disease, the fibrous
roots and stems, the nodes—
the areas between. Words broke
through the atmosphere like weeds—

carcinoma, sarcoma, leukemia,
lymphoma. In the steamy air
we grew red periwinkle and mayapple—
plants the book said might contain
the cure—offered them to her. Mother,

in her shrunken body too high
on prednisone to reach,
sat in her over-
sized chair—needles blooming
from her porta catheter, while the iron tree
with its sack liquid leaves
stayed still against the swell
of her face—peaked sun.
The wind held its breath.
No one spoke

of death. Outside,
the ornamental grass grew plumes—
clumps of hope, spiked promises
of more life. In this false transfusion

of light, we huddled around her
as if she were the only heat.

The Baobab Tree I

The sun will not leave
you alone. Day after day it comes to stare
with its drying eye, pinpoints its beam

on the trunk of your larynx, fixates
on the flower of your voice, the fruit
of your phrase. Today you are

so hoarse and the burnt look
of the skin beneath your neck scalds
my own. I've come to join you here,

Mother, in this desert—
on this hot and grassy plain, our bodies seared
above the ground. Above the ground

you are so pleasing to the bats that circle
at night—so many seeds still left
in your mealy pulp. How you thrust

your ropey arms upward into the immobile air,
trying and trying to get along
with that seething, unreachable tumor.

Perennial

So what if next year the deep pink burst
will not appear outside my door.
What if, after all the tending,

the IVs filled with said miracles—droplets
from the blood bags that reawaken your body,
ignite your mind—your face,
a blossom, will not appear outside my door?
Today, June peonies lighten my path—so what

if next year they do not come back? If
they do and you do not,
I'll hack them down with an ax—
that they dare reappear,
their spread petals wild tongues
screaming SO WHAT?

Cycle of Sound

Hickory, dickory, dock—
it began of course in the nursery.
Mouth so safe—the tucked-in
repetitions that would make
a child smile, absurd words—
how I loved the non-
sense. *The mouse*

ran up the clock.
Then, *the clock struck one.*
The chemotherapy is working.
Her hair has not yet fallen
to the dried-out ground—just thins.
I sit and listen

as she retells her life's stories—hear only
the fragile rhythms. The notes expand
then stick together. The accordion of her
years fans then shrinks to a small space.
The music and the place
will remain here after

conversation is over. I run
down there every afternoon to check
the minute and the hour
hands, the drum and the pendulum, the weight—

to reverse the escapement.
The mouse ran down,
the mouse ran up. She's trapped

inside the ticking clock,
and I flail against the break-
proof glass, not able to get her out.
As ridiculous as it sounds

hickory, dickory, dock.

Manic

I love the beat of the sick blood
through the sad heart—

how I monitor each sound,
your half-smile and girl-
ish giggle rising above
the small mountain
of pills next to your bed.
I love how the word *re-*

mission bubbles out
of my mouth, my infantile
flourish of inexact adjectives
when someone asks how you are.
I love all
the sentiments in the "Get Well"

cards—bad poetry
that communicates, fills
my head. Heady, I listen to soft
rock on the radio. Manic, I do

a U-turn on the River Styx.
Whoosh, Here We Go. I tell you
you are my passenger as we travel
against the current. Neil

Diamond sings—shines on, on
my speedy flip tongue.

Baby's Breath

All summer I followed the angel, followed
her following the path that finally broke apart
as it reached past the heat of August.
The sun that warmed her small curved shoulders turned

its head and laughed, began its retreat
no matter how she begged—showed it
the hundred transfusion bags,
the chemicals that could now kill
hope. Naked, all fat dropped from her flesh
with nothing to hold on to, she showed it
her bald soul. I saw her do so

in the mirror, while I cradled her head, combed
what was left. She rocked back and forth
as I touched the dried Baby's Breath.
Fall had entered the room, but she would not
yet give up. The light grew

so thin and in the distance the sun
laughed, and I could not understand.

Heat

Soon the dazed glory heat will be replaced by leaves—
dry silence will eclipse your voice.
The bleached-out grass readies itself—accepts
its patches, awaits its white winter wig.
Yours is propped on a plastic head
atop your dresser. I stare at it—its eyeless
face—your future. I almost cannot find you,

Mother, as we wobble into the deep
humidity—the air that suffocates.
It is the coffin season—everything closing
in on us as I take you out to tea,
to eat our little Russian cakes and tiny crust-
less sandwiches—our portions

getting smaller, our time together petite and quaint
as the menu offered. *And we take it.* Observe
the fragile vase on the table
filled with delicate flowers.
Outside, they'd die quick in this end-

of-summer temperature. Remember this hot
moment, I say to myself, its blazing
touch—how it burns into my sight
for when you are not.

Lizard

You grew so thin your bracelet slipped
off your wrist. We couldn't find it
in the windblown sand—
our eyes encrusted, almost blind—
combs that once lifted your thick hair fell
and were buried there. The lizard slid

along and was adorned with many ornaments—
throat fans, tail crests, casques on its head,
spines and frills around its throat.
It grew so large and corpulent
as it ate you up. We knew
no chant to drive it out.
On our knees,

we watched it probe and dig.
Straightened, we raced after it.
It was so capable of rapid acceleration.
We chased it through the hospital.
Then, in June they scanned you
with their enormous machines
and it was nowhere to be seen.
We picked huge bouquets of summer

flowers and you smiled. We shopped
for new clothes to cover your delicate translucent
bones. In the dressing room I saw your soul.

The lizard had chewed away all fat and left you
luminous. The three-way mirror
almost captured it. But in the fall

its venom began to spew again
from the longitudinal groove
on the inner side
of each mandibular tooth.
Oh I knew its body well—
its chameleon ways were no
surprise—the hell in

all its designs. The last
time it rose up on the screen
I wept and screamed. Cold-
blooded, how it craved your hot, dry
body—your fever that it sunned itself

under. Gorged, it's gone on hidden
folds of skin—sails to glide it
through the air. No one knows exactly where
it will land.

Guardian

In a brush of fine plumes,
beyond the edge of the sun,
against that disk, there exist

intense ribbons of flame
that look like the ones you wound
into the tips of my braids.

You'd kiss the lush top of my head
(not yet thinned by adult dreads)—
a blessing, you said. In the high

arches of the photosphere
violent convection plaits and shifts
ions and electrons into streaming

patterns. How I'd scream
and fling my sash
when you did not tie it tight enough.

I wanted to bind myself
to that cloth—to you.
Now, in the telescope

I look for the spot of greatest magnetic
strength, press my face against the glass—
O bright filament

about to completely vanish.

Petit Point I

Take half a stitch each day
with silk thread slightly thicker
than a hair and years to complete
the picture. As many as 3,122
points to the square
inch are possible with the aid
of a magnifying glass. Remember,
it takes years. Consider it:

the suture—the needle—passed into
one skin edge through the full
depth of the hole and out the other
end. For deep wounds (and they will
come) pass the needle through twice,
first shallowly, then plumb.
When the trauma is greater

use a sterile strand of catgut
and loop it so it is caught
in the adjacent loop.
(Are you getting the picture?
Perhaps not.) Think
of how the furrier works
with the stink of the dead
animal laid out on the table
before him, stitching flesh

by piercing first one margin
of the incision and then the other
from within outward, overlying

sutures placed through
the seromuscular layers
to reinforce the closure—
CLOSE HER. CLOTHE HER. please.
(Now, you're getting the weave of it.) In

intestinal surgery the needle
passes through all layers of bowel
and the loop of suture material
is made to fall over the point
(WHAT'S THE POINT? SHE DIED ANYWAY.)
of emergence (the soul?)
when it comes up
and forms the self-

locking stitch, pulled
taut. *Like Death.*
Rent of the abdomen—sick purse,
she can't eat, can't even finish
a dish of small peas—petit point
of hunger. How lost

she looks in the large quilted
bed jacket while underneath
the scratchy sheets lies the primary
gash with its knotted everted
tissue held together to prevent
any disruption of the evisceration.

Her body is so neatly
punctured, then put back
together—delicate container
of such loveliness
lying there before
the surgeon, the tailor, the artist.

Conclusion I

I carried a full tray
of food, incense bowl, libation cup—
bread for the gods, sweet odors
for the Lord—kneeled
at the altar. No one was there.
I looked for anyone
who could help, tried to make
my presence felt, climbed
onto the stone table
as if I were a sheep or an ox.
There were no sacrificial stakes—
no cosmic trees or shallow pits
where sacred flames could be lit,
only me spread there alone
under the fire of the sun.

appassionata

Mother in Summer II

You became the lightest of the elements—
all hydrogen—your heart
equal to the mass of the sun and he,
in his summer white suit,
black shirt, white tie, your match
in fever. For months it was the day
of the solstice—that tilt of Earth
at the tropic of Cancer,
the longest expanse of light.
The longest disease of dark
an unnoticeable part

widening slowly in the humidity.
Here, he was the southern wind
blown in, encircling your face, the land
of your body. *O lava of passion.*
Did it ever become too much,
burn your flesh to raw nerves,
your mind to scorched and cracked?
Or was that the legacy for a daughter
to inherit? Deep inside

the planet skull so many desires
flame and orbit.
How can they not escape
into volcanoes that erupt?

But you were so quiet, so private—
never boiling even one word. All anger
inward—the rage
a wild cell starting

its own small world. He entered
and the atoms and the molecules twirled
faster and faster and you,
a snowflake in summer, spun
and broke apart—past water.
Then, you recaptured yourself,
not to frozen like your mother,
just a bit frostbit—numbed at the tips—
unlike your daughter always a splash
on the cement.
He came and went

thinking you'd be there
for life, warming his earth,
neither of you knowing
that kind of weather
doesn't lift easily and pass
back through the atmosphere
leaving it untouched.

Muff . . .

made from a piece of her
mouton coat, I'd put my hands snugly in-
to it. I was so safe
with her sitting next to me on the bus.
How fast we passed the hospital, the funeral
home, the cemetery, on our way
to buy new shoes.
Time fluffed—an endless warm cylinder
of muff, animal coat held so close

to my heart. Her mother rode
with us—her face a shard.
I'd force my mind to round,
then stuff it into my muff—
good hiding place.
My mother sat so quiet in the soft,
cheap fur—life no longer lived, lived
in my cheeks as I brushed against
the plush. Twins we were in a winter flush

of happiness, or so I thought,
but the chill in her mother's satchel
that she lugged across the ocean,
she dragged onto the land.

No skin could thaw the heavy
freeze we slipped into—how soon
it bruised, then cracked, each
brand-new pair of shoes.

In the Beginning . . .

it was an evening clutch,
a melon wedge of pink
satin and diamanté trim.
It sat in my left hand—the moon

not yet a full-blown explosion.
The nights held dainty
hopes of a kiss, an arm around
my waist, an accidental brush against
my breasts—hard and sugar
colored, no psychedelic bruises yet.
No "mock croc" or "fake snake" existed, no

joke of "a silk purse
from a sow's ear" pertained, no
dissolution of skin to gelatin
from which fiber dyed red
could be spun and loomed. It *can* be done.
It did happen. Inside the striking

exterior the flesh can overheat and melt
into oblivion. Passion makes it possible—
the half-moon only half

the narration, the other half
yet to come. *In the beginning . . .*

"it was an evening clutch,
a melon wedge of pink satin . . ."

Petit Point II

When the air is calm and on
clear nights with the wind so light,
dewdrops form inside the hollows
of the grass between its joints
like kisses of small measure.
Certainly better than the deposit
which takes the shape of hoarfrost
or when the temperature falls low enough

to stitch flakes together into hex-
agonal patterns. When water molecules
conjoin, that violence
can sculpt a rigid lattice.
However beautiful and intricate

the fallen snow, if it survives the spring
and then the summer, it will
turn to ice and then to glacier.
And all avalanches of passion
will not bring even
a petit point of pleasure.

Larch

I've learned to exist like the larch,
patiently waiting for the ice to melt
in the ultra-short summer—

a little liquid sufficient
for the drawn-out winter
when it keeps its head frozen solid.
I know I am so safe

with you in this familiar place.
And when someone comes along—
a hot brute wind—
that blows me open, I only lose

a handful of hairs. Tear and surrender
them for analysis under
a magnifying glass. How bent and split
each appears. Thick and warped

and lovely tree with needs
whittled to bonsai dimensions,
I know too well
how long you have lived
so near the cold Pole.

Relief

The morning is high with young air.
What does it know from the old wind,
the crackle of leaves, sad notes
about beauty—the hours perfumed

by pastels, then violent reds?
The blood lily with its fleshy stem
tempts me to lie down with it
in the afternoon's thick grass.
Tonight a tea rose will tear

at its own delicate throat, spread
itself too wide over
the path where lovers are all
mouths—their tongues all

pistils and stamens—while you and I
brush against each other's
lips, call it a kiss.
We look forward with familiar

relief that September arrives almost
tomorrow. Soon there will be less
heat to remind us of what we miss.

The Baobab Tree II

As if dead, it drops
its leaves and waits through
the long droughts, the life-bringing
rain soaked into the soft wood
of its smooth and shiny bark. *Touch*

my skin, I say, silently.
My limbs are branches wildly blown
onto the bed—moist
thoughts buried deep next to the bone.
I've adapted well to dry
land. Even outside

there's been no snow.
The children stand in last August's grass
with their makeshift sleds and hope,
while the old just talk and talk
about past wet and cozy winters
they do not quite remember. Far away

the Baobab tree survives
no matter what the weather,
while here we crave the sudden coming
of the new year—perhaps a storm—to re-
assure us that we'll thrive, or at least
make us believe we're still alive.

Bald

Summer's crown thins, the scalp
of Earth covers with a wist-
ful down—no more exuberant
activity. The strands left

on the pillow are too noticeable. Will you
touch my breasts, or do you prefer
just to lie next to me and
rest? Dormant? Dead?
What is left to harvest? I gather

the remains at the apex
of my skull, rub the stubs,
touch the bald spot
I've dug out. In the center

of the sun—that maelstrom
of hot plasma—a dark coronal hole
offers an escape for the solar wind.
At night, I pick my violent
head to tunnel out a path for the trapped

sick spirit. Here it is
autumn again with its worn
lust and lone deep circular want
to just return home.

Archangel

She makes her meal of anti-
depressants, transfusions, chemicals.
Her scalp bears fragile tufts—
dandelion fluff disseminated
by the wind. The magic

formulae for protection from demons
carved in olive wood and covered with gold
from the innermost part of the Temple,
she places in my inky hands.
I am writing about God and the angel

with the flaming sword He positioned
at the gate of Eden to guard it after
the expulsion. Who will keep me
from the snake

when she is gone? Her winged
head grows so strong.
I bring her slippers for her birth-
day, a size too large—
her feet so small.
Once she could clear a path

good enough for me to follow.
I pulled out my hair—
made a tonsure just like hers—
sacred spots the world could not
touch. Only us.
We covered them with barrettes and clips
and felt safe. Now I can barely

find her when I enter her room.
Soon, only my pen will draw her in.

Head

Fragments of the crown in the comb—
scabs of scalp where the decoration
insists on controlled
seductiveness. Teeth inserted,
forced into curls,
buns, rolls, or scant
tresses increased by switches
or rats—forms of more locks
to pad the head.
Open fans, ovals, pyramids,
spread wings, horseshoes, scallops,
semi or full circles—rhapsodies
of trim to tiara the brain.
Attempts to contain
perversions of thought—
perfectly coiffed hair pinned
down. All illusions of shape
over an unknowable space.

The meat knife did not cut
the skin of the scalp—that glazed mound
smooth as the face of the tiny clock,
time I can cover with my thumb.

The minute and the hour hands
look like stubs of hair
I could rub out. I could have

dug deeper, dove into the bottomless
dream of the release of blood.
The body is such a polluted sack,
but the head, that sick historic globe,
is what I long to lance, cleanse

with a sword. It is a war
I cannot win. It is a place
I cannot reach—this world
that cannot be leeched.

Low brush dominated by heaths,
proteas, sedges, rushes—jumbled
landforms of pines find refuge
in the desert of my scalp.
I don't pull out all the needles—
some escape my will-
ful hands. The damage

I view with bifocals, two mirrors,
and a jeweler's loop pressed against my crown,
while you look down on me like God
and count the nubs—today nineteen,
same as yesterday and tomorrow.
This is the way we make love. How long

will the hair grow after we die—
survive in the deep
underground river, the thorns
finally bearing full fruit?
Who will see this? Know to bless it?
The garden finally returned, untouched.

I scrape my scalp with the brass
comb—the one with Cupid
in the act of rescuing a heart or soul.
It barely holds my thinned crown.
Perhaps a fragile tortoise one
with floral foliate would be more fitting
or something more somber, even

funereal. Sunk-in teeth
are the trouble—hard
and blunt like those in the mouth
that break sound, scratch
the tongue with their chipped edges—
acid lies pushing out the pumped-up
lips. *O Eros how you destroy lives.*
How theatrical

my tiara with its band of raised
beading and cupolas—a dog-headed
fish supports the sea. The symbolism
as obtuse as I.

Chameleons

The desert is too hot for comfort
and the lizard waits in the shade
or under the sand—its clawed
toes dug in. I try to skip over it—
try so hard not to be tripped—
but my tongue does not fit exact
and quiet in my mouth. I try

to settle myself with silence—
become more chameleon—
but the environment changes faster
than my repertoire of colors
so I show
my thoughts and get caught
in a tangle of hisses. Nine days

after All Fools' Day,
when small animals begin their small
crawls from their small holes,
the lizard reappears in all its scaled

splendor. Nightmare of my heart, again

how you hold me in your jaw
anticipating the swallow
as soon as you feel my familiar
giving up of the struggle.

Each eye moves separately, signals
me into confusion, contradiction—
happy hateful looks, simultaneous.
Days it likes to lie on the lawn absorbing
heat from the sun—warming itself to well
beyond the temperature of the air
I breathe. In the dark I hear

its sounds, smell the odors from its inner
thighs, let it grasp the thin skin
of mine with its toe fans—
their chevron-shaped edges digging in.
The hemipenis inverts and inserts.
Copulation lasts between fifteen minutes
and a few seconds. Sometimes it just rams

its rotating head into the dirt,
burrows there for hours, then climbs
the vertical panes of glass to my nighttime
window to watch me undress,
comb my hair—touch the tender tips
of stubble where I've twisted
out the long strands. Its own brushlike
setae help it cling, while waiting motionless
for purchase. I've felt the shooting
of the sticky tongue, cannot rid myself
of the image of its jaw—the increased gape—
as it pulled me down. How it loves

to devour the fallen, tender
fruit and leaf and flower.

Reentering the Scar

I said *no* to opening the tangled
mass of arteries, capillaries, veins.
How the blood begged for the rush. I wanted
to maintain a certain integrity
of skin—forget about the odd pleasures
of intrusion. I dug my nails into the fine grooves
in my hands, held together
my legs. Although my surface sickened
with each weakening negative—an eczema
patched my brain, a warty place
scaled with indecision. You entered

with French Pruners, Poacher's Spade, Singing
Grass Shears, a Single-Seat Kneeler
guaranteed not to rust, corrode,
dent, your eye bent on mine—
wet and too delicate. In your pocket you carried

galvanized wire and a copper marker that en-
graves so easily with ballpoint pen
and over time acquires
a beautiful verdigris patina.
With all this you could not miss the flower.
You thought with your Classic Hoe

how could I possibly say *no.*
Now, in bruised silence, I use herbal infusions—

chamomile, red clover, rose
petals combined with oils of lavender, geranium.
The scar has faded from last year
and the one from the year before, minuscule.
For this moment, how I glisten.

The Interior of the Sun I

In this most powerful place beyond
the thin wrinkled skin of Earth,
at this core, it will take a million years
for my fever to reach your face.

No more offerings when I gaze up.

Helios with his chariot and Re
sailing his boat across the sky
have disappeared at this apex
of heat among huge clouds of gases and dust.

How my cheeks burst scarlet
last week when I sat across
from you, the sun
lit the table. Your bright
eyes glowed and gave glimpses
of an untainted climate—language
dazzling with kindness or so it seemed—
god whom I cannot contain.

Gone

Without the solar flare I starve,
yet I let them place the lead apron
over me as if it were a blanket—
curl into the weight of it.
And if this doesn't work they talk
of a thick shield of concrete
to protect me from high

energy. I am so finally quiet.
The alpha and the beta
rays and the subatomic
particles penetrated my body.
Where are you now?
I stayed so close to the cellular

phone—twenty-four hours a day.
The women who painted radium watch and clock
dials grew weak, dizzy, nauseous—
it's all in the medical texts. The heat

from last summer was impossibly hot.
Hit me, I whispered.
Afterward, you offered polluted
tap water, which I drank.
The newscaster warned to boil it.

Then you asked, *Is there anything else
you want? Marry me,* I wept.
The cosmic radiation

was too much. First, you laughed,
then you left.

Perihelion

If only you would fade
into the sparklings that punctuate
this blank of space, today
could vanish more easily. I
come so close,

ironic in my bundling
up against the ice, while underneath
my thighs glisten—wet from the press
of my skin, your shine

on me, star of unexceptional size
who could almost disappear
alongside any hot blue giant.
Millions of you could fit inside
Antares—red monster of my next
heart. My lips

are frostbit when we're at
our nearest. Numb from
your quiet, I ask if I was
ever your focus, lift
my face to your face,
beg for your cold kiss.

With the Earth's elliptical
orbit closest to the sun, in full view
of the young moon, two days from
the Twelfth Night when the debris
from the Yule feast must be cleared,
before the quarter moon when firewood
must be cut to keep it from snapping,

I see your burning
face, exact in memory—
that tilted place. On this slippery
unsafe day when it's best to stay in,
the icy windows are lit by the birth of the son
of the Egyptian sky goddess. *They say*

your mother, too, was powerful
and beautiful. I've seen pictures
and it's true, but she didn't love you well—
sin always on her kissy
lips, poisoning your shining
child skin. When I get this near

there is less rage than after
you spread my legs with your knees—
never asking please—just wanting
and taking, covering me
with your chilling blaze
and me unable to breathe,
trying this minute
to spin and spin away.

Spinning in disbelief, I rotated
around her globed head—all visible
light and heat. Bright eye
of day, radiant flux of energy,
her surface glowed unblemished
except for the dead

hair follicles I tried to wipe off
with a damp towel.
Today I came so close
to kiss that space

where she's come to exist, but dust
clogged my throat, sealed
lash to lash. Blinded,
I cried into the lost

wind—last breath—
Mother, now center of drought and ice,
you have eclipsed my lover,
you have eclipsed my life.

The Interior of the Sun II

It is the dream of reentering
Eden—innocent and running
up three flights of stairs
through the back door
into the kitchen.
They are all there:
Grandmother, Mother, Grandpa, Father.
No death here—not yet—no
lymph glands have swelled, buckled
the skin, lungs easily inhale
the fragrance from the thick brisket
steaming in the pot.
No one yet coughs. The blood

clot in Father's heart is
only a metaphor for
a child's loss. Later, she'll beg
her most violent lover to hit her
down there. Up

here dinner's almost ready. The flowered
oilcloth sweats on the Formica,
while she can't wait to watch the fire-
flies attach and electrify against
the scorched window screen.
How she loves to singe

her fingertips with its prison pattern.
Her grandmother will scream
that now she must again go wash.
Will she ever get clean of the burnt-
out center of others' lives? *Hit me,*

she whispered last night
to her lover. *There,* pointing
to the wiry pit. How it fascinates—
the way the two of them mix

up love with hate. When he bites
her nipples to blood,
she can almost hear him cry
to his dead mama.
Hers just sits quiet and bald,
a million miles away. Chemotherapy
is doing its trick.
The trick is hope

that when she opens
the next door, they'll all be standing there—
waiting for her. She's come in
from play. It's summer again
and someone loves her.

Lavender

I've created a man, tell you
he's majestic like the giant
Allium that grows and grows
outside my window—
how I love the tall stem
crowned with the burst of purple.
I crave to hold it in my mouth,
then swallow it like the oval
pill I cradle on my tongue—
lavender, my mother's favorite color.
I wrapped her bald head in it,
learned to make the perfect turban.
I tell you his name is *Michael* and how well
he makes me feel, how he carries me in-

to calm. Your worst word lashings cut less
into my synapses. My serotonin rises
and I smile. He comes to my door
clothed in full armor, carrying
chains to bind the devil.
Inside my brain your voice
remains, but slowly it dries

like last week's peonies—blown-out
blisters shrinking in the sun
as the lump in her neck once did.

Soon the hardy lilies
will make their stately bow.
Michael will make of them a bouquet
I'll allow into my body.

Oh the miracle of the pills.

Conclusion II

I looked up and saw the meticulous way
you knotted the rope to the basket,
lowered it into the mountainous cave
where I'd fallen. I ate

the bread and, strengthened, climbed
through the slosh of wasted flesh, bodies of bone.
You smiled at the tomb's mouth,
dressed in the gold of the imperial court—
or was it just a simple long coat?
I don't remember much except
how you warmed me with your arms—
wings? I became so vague—

firelike and vaporous. You whispered,
It's not time to weigh your soul
and held me loose
enough to let me go. That night
when you appeared, I saw you lift the stars.

lacrimosa

Mother in Summer III

I imagine it is wool pulled
from a dead or diseased sheep
that covers you—dyed
the primary color with the longest
wavelength of light. My eye can reach
no farther. Beyond this red
the visible world ends and the spirit

takes over. The healthy yolk of the soul—
the one that's blessed with an oily
substance that protects
from flash floods of primal thoughts—
I have lost. Shriveled,
it's blown somewhere onto a barren
patch of earth.
Even a cool downpour of rain
would leave me just drenched

with my parched mind—
wondering how long cloth lasts,
not flesh, inside the vault.
Enough time has passed
so that all that's there
may be bones and fibers
that mat and interlock
under the heat and the moisture
and the pressure.

Comb

The tortoise comb—
the one with the couple in the garden
complete with willow tree
(my mother asked to be buried without
her wig or any ornament)—
has a pagoda in the background,
a sampan approaching, and a low border
of flowers, buds, and leaves.
(She left when the leaves were alarmed with color.
Days before, we sat in the car
and drank black coffee.
She wore a red cotton hat
trimmed with a fake white carnation.
It almost hid her bald head.)
The comb is of the Ch'ing dynasty, 18th century.
The Chinese peonies are calm and lovely.
A lady with thick, rich hair and a wealthy
lover must have owned it
as he owned her. Perhaps,
it was returned at the end
of the affair, or her death.
Now a museum exhibits it.
(My mother left each of her daughters
three items of her jewelry.

She wrote the list of who should have what
two years before the final time
she got sick. She didn't own
a fancy comb though I wish she had
and left it to me.)
If it were mine, I'd keep it
on my crown, even underneath the ground.

Falling

The [falling] observer is therefore justified
in considering his state as one of "rest."
—Albert Einstein

That day last fall
how graceful the gulls
rose, then dipped
back to the sand.
We predicted where
each would land—
the sun a blazing coin
we could pocket.
The white birch leaves

glistened—you called them *golden*
and told me to *look.*
Instead, I turned toward you
as we sat in the car,
memorizing that we were
here. The depth of the deep

cold blue expanse of lake
did not seem an omen
then, as we planned
next week's outing. Where
we would go. Be
together. Mother. While

a space in another place
was slowly being opened
by men whose eyes avert the sun—
their faces focused forever down.
There, we'd fall
in fewer days than the number
of fingers on two hands. In prayer
I'd let them lower you
into the hole,
too numb to feel the final crash.

That day I just drifted
through what was expected.

Petit Point III

When the days and nights were of equal length
and the autumn equinox warned
the birds to migrate toward the equator
to escape the falling temperatures, we drove
up and down a single block—landlocked—
and watched the leaves in their last dance

of color. How flushed and fevered
they were in their final daze—
a petit point of terror, their panic
sewn into the strict canvas
of nature, the extreme stage

in the fear sequence before us.
The plummet toward Earth's crust
where all becomes organic litter—
the dream over—was days away.
Reel and keel. Past topsoil
and humus, the interlock
with silt and sand and fragments
called *parent material*

came so fast, the zero
down to unweathered bedrock—
a place where you are now woven
into an indecipherable, invisible pattern.

Frigid

It is the season of frozen
water—tears of sleet, tears
of snow, hail of grief.
Some plants die
and leave their seeds,
so it is with you and me.
I lie dormant, almost dead,
these glacial mornings

in bed. I brought you pudding
during the fall, on the vermilion border
of your lips I saw it
cling—every detail of your being

noticed, the downward twist
of fingernails, eyelids thin and luminous.
The last time we touched, someone
had shut them. I tried to reach past

your fading surface,
to the stopped warm heart I spoke.
Mother. Please. Mother.
(mother still mother
never more
quiet.) *I'll bring you back
with my pen,* no matter

how cold my worn-out hand.
Frigid and glum in this icy

life, I'll try like the larch
to ignore the brute indifference
of the blank winter sun—
the punch of existence.

How chilling it is
with me here and you there.

Untouched

Massage of words, orgasms
of thoughts—when I touch
my pen too much
motion happens. The fabric red

you are wrapped in, inflames. Dead
follicles of hair, detritus—burnt
grains—offerings to small gods encrust
my brain. When I combed
the bald scalp

that was your crown,
you closed your eyes
and said, *It feels so good.*
It was all
I could do. We were

rhythmic—you in bed
and me standing, standing
the sight of what was left
of us. Today the first snow covers
you, seals you farther
from my reach—my hands

that a few weeks ago could cradle
your head—bundled in soft
pink. Now you're dressed
in too deep

a color. Flushed, we rocked—
you told me so—as you sang
of how I frightened you.
Baby girl, what do I do with you?
I don't want you to break
so I'll not touch you too much.
I don't want to make any mistake.
That's how I felt when you grew

so fragile. How I wanted to hold
on to you, my arms ached, then numbed,
I didn't want to make any mistake,
fearful that you'd crumble—
tear like the skin
this feral pen writes on.

Red

These shrunken days I long
to die, to crawl back-
ward to your womb—sad vault

which now is forever locked.
Death grabbed the key—
never to give up

its privacy. Oh how
I love a secret. Except this.
Accept this,

say the rabbi, the minister, the priest.
Why? Why in these leaves
flame to ash

did you pick *that color?*
Was it something you saw
in our last ride together—

the bleeding autumn oak
filling you with hope,
readying your body to start over,

return your firstborn
to her primordial bed? I rush
into my pillow and dream of being crushed

by *red.* Everything burns
with it—the trees, the sun,
my voice. Whatever you were

celebrating by that choice—
heralding in—I want
to be part of it, Mother.

Breach

The large-headed fetus rests so well
in the rounded and capacious birth
canal—the sciatic notch wide and A-
shaped. How I long to shrink, to fit
into that hollowed basin complex

of bones—start again. Breach
time and space—all forces
I've been taught to accept,
pray to, and respect.
Each morning I awaken

too sad to the sun's indifferent request
to get up. Shrouded in ice, lying
in his sky-frozen coffin, he barely
cares to arouse me, nor I him.
Season of seduction, gone. No warmth

here, anywhere, except perhaps in her
body's old scar—thick and fibrous.
Closed wound—open up. Womb
gently laid to rest within the vault,
take me back—*open up.*

The Baobab Tree III

I hid in its wet hollowed trunk,
used it for liquid and shelter.
I called it *Mother.*
It stood strong against the sun
with branches spread yards beyond
its bulging womb. I slept
beneath oblong fruit and knew the promise
of food. Somewhere else it was

cold, the air so dry my spirit had split
my skin. No balm could calm it.
I sat and wrote about it
in my room while she shivered
in her tomb—first winter

without her. I remembered
she told me how she wanted to come back
as a tree so I climbed

inside the oddest one,
where I knew I belonged.

Of May

My palm recalls how it was to touch
the comb to your scalp—
most of the hair fallen out.
You'd close your eyes to the day
and say how good
it felt. It was near the end

of May that the ripe grass
was too thick—except for the new strands
that pushed through the mud.
Some wisps curled around my fingertips
like a kiss. Some were
still stubs—awful needles
of grief that refused to grow

into acceptance. Other visitors brought
sunlit bouquets, talked easily
to the flat ground, lay
on their sides among the graves,
while I was so obvious—upright, I cried,
Mother, what are you doing here?
It is the height of spring, please
take me outside, outside of here
let's name the flowers, name

the leaves. It was too soon
for reason, too early
for us in this florid forever-
returning season.

Grief

Clumsy thumb of sadness—
opposable digit, how stiffly it drops
the delicate mind onto the concrete.
If only there were a pocket
deep enough to hide it
like the huge one inside
her swing coat—bright cloth.
I was waist high to her
and the waste of her before my eyes
was years beyond my vision.
Once I left my thumb
in an open door
and someone (not her) came along
and slammed it shut.
My nail snapped off
and blood drowned the linoleum.
Now the loss of her leaves a stain
on every floor.
I stood there screaming and stunned,
while she dove in and found the nail—
that hardened plate of cells—
and tried to stick it back on,
but we were just left
with the devastated flesh.

She chose a red suit with minute pockets
that could never hold the unending
picture of that violent color
spilt over her stilled body.
In the starless night
my hand has lost all grace.
I only feel the awful cut.
I watched the nail
slowly begin again. Near the root
a white crescent shape rose up.

Return

The flowers are so redundant
in their persistent return.
I watch their dance beneath the sun—
push then spread, spread then push—
they'll do anything to get its attention.
Today, I dress in shocking

pink—hope you'll catch
the full flush of my peony face.
It is June, *what did you expect?*
I say to myself,
what did *you* expect?
I've come back more

alone, burning under
memory's bright heat.
Much has been
lost: a mother who just left
me this blazing

sweater, a too-fevered
lover. I feel the press
of the root. The humus that surrounds
my heart insists
on this flamboyant notice.

Silkworms

The mulberry tree stood dead—
all of its leaves attacked
by small white heads
that swung themselves
from side to side in compulsive
figure eights creating the image
of infinity. *I could go on*

like this forever. Once
I nested with her.
We created uneven double threads
never to be separated,
or so we thought,
like the ones that made up
her blouse I would borrow—
that she chose—
with its softly knotted texture.
It had a bow at the neck.
Someone had tied it well enough.
She looked like a gift

being sent to a distant place.
All fluid drained out, now
we flutter over each other
endlessly, like moths.

The Interior of the Sun III

Deep within the skull flames
the pineal gland—sweet pea, third eye,
soul seat—how I dig down
to you day and night,
my raw fingertips rubbing a sad patch
of scalp to larger

infection. Remember the festering lovers
who scalded each other with light;
they became so crisp with hate
they never touched again.
Each wanted to outsmart
the other, be as powerful as the sun—
sky borne or layered inside the cranium,

either way it's way out
of reach. So why even try
to read the books
on science, philosophy, religion?
They won't tell you more
than television with its absolute
burnt hole of no information.
The rabbi asked me not to speak

at my mother's funeral,
said I should mourn silently,

then handed me a shovel to toss
dirt on what I'd just lost. *Star*
light, star bright, tell me
where you are tonight—holy fire
in the center of my brain or out there
bold beam, drifting?

Conclusion III

Violet shot silk, edged with ruching.
Gathered pocket with nothing in it. Knotted
Bag. White satin embroidered with bright
thread, tamboured with spangles
that swing no matter how sad

the hand that holds it.
Green velvet with glass stitched
into it. Imitation ivory frame
with press button catch. *Gathered pocket*
with nothing in it. Day
Bag. Soft kid with pastel piped petals
that look almost

edible. *Gathered pocket*
with nothing in it. Twilight
Bag. Corded rayon with gilt
metal on which a painted tea rose
is half-scratched away
with the hard tip of a nervous
nail. *Gathered pocket*

with nothing in it. Night
Bag. With gasmask circa 1939.

Cream twilled cotton with man-made
fiber. Figured in yellow
viscose, a pattern
of gazelles, panthers, flowers—
life—short carrying
handles. Easy to open
just in case. Encased
to protect—diffuse
every aftereffect, though
the small print reads
NOT FOR ACTUAL USE.

About the Author

Susan Hahn is a poet, a playwright, and the editor of *Tri-Quarterly* magazine. She has published four books of poetry, most recently *Holiday,* and is the recipient of numerous awards for poetry including the Society of Midland Authors Award, the George Kent Prize from *Poetry* magazine, and many Illinois Arts Council awards.